Palm Sunday Parade

Martha McKown

CSS Publishing Company, Inc.
Lima, Ohio

PALM SUNDAY PARADE

Copyright © 1995 by
CSS Publishing Company, Inc.
Lima, Ohio

You may copy the material in this publication if you are the original purchaser, for use as it was intended (worship material for worship use; educational material for classroom use; dramatic material for staging and production). No additional permission is required from the publisher for such copying by the original purchaser only. Inquiries should be addressed to: CSS Publishing Company, Inc., 517 South Main Street, P.O. Box 4503, Lima, Ohio 45802-4503.

Scripture quotations are from the *New Revised Standard Version of the Bible,* copyright 1989 by the Division of Christian Education of the National Council of the Churches of Christ in the USA. Used by permission.

ISBN 0-7880-0322-4   PRINTED IN U.S.A.

*To Leslie,
My Husband*

PREFACE

Even when I was a little girl I had a strong sense of the drama of worship. As a director of Christian education and a local church pastor, I have tried to wed people's affections and the dynamic presence of the Living God, often doing this through drama.

With complex schedules, church people find it difficult to take time for drama that involves much memory and long rehearsals. Realizing this I have written and directed dramas that require a minimum of practice time.

May your use of this worship drama be an experience of communication with God. May your congregation of God's people find it another way to the heart of God.

INSTRUCTIONS

This drama is written to be used in the sanctuary for the Palm Sunday worship. It may involve children and youth and adults.

PERSONS:
    Narrator
    Voice 1
    Voice 2
    Voice 3
    First Speaker
    Second Speaker
    Third Speaker
    Fourth Speaker
    Fifth Speaker
    Voice 4
    Voice 5
    Voice 6
    A chorus of children and youth

Some of these may be combined. They may dress in regular clothes or biblical-looking tunics and robes. One microphone may be used, but several would be more effective.

The chorus should have helium-filled, multi-colored balloons or streamers of colorful cloth. They should wear their most colorful clothes.

HYMNS FOR CHORUS AND CONGREGATION:
    1. "Love Divine, All Loves Excelling," by Wesley and Zundel

    2. "Tell Me The Stories Of Jesus" by Parker and Callinor or "All Glory, Laud, And Honor" by Theodulph of Orleans and Teschner

3. "Come, Christians, Join To Sing" by Bateman or "Ask Ye What Great Thing I Know" by Herbert and Vaughan Williams or "Rejoice Ye Pure In Heart" by Phemptre and Messiter.

SERVICE MUSIC:
Prelude, postlude and offertory may be a piano with flute or violin.
Offertory music suggestions: "Jesu, Joy Of Man's Desiring" by Bach or "Blow Ye The Trumpet, Blow" by Edson.

PROPS:
Very few props are necessary for this drama. Balloons or cloth streamers are needed, but costumes are optional. Players feel their parts more in costume.

Make it a joyous beginning of Holy Week!

The Earth Sings Praise

Martha McKown
Moderately quick
French Folk Song

We will praise you, Dear God,
Were we to be qui - et,
Let us dance Ho - san - nas!

for your gift to us,
things a - round would shout,
to ex - press glad joy,

Im - man - uel was with us,
Their glad songs would rain down,
Com - ing from the whole earth,

God in Je - sus came.
rush - ing as a stream.
sound of ju - bi - lee.

PALM SUNDAY PARADE

A Palm/Passion Sunday worship for children and youth

NARRATOR: Welcome, People of God . . . . Palm Sunday, crowds gathered in Jerusalem. On a hillside outside the holy city a group followed their leader toward the city and the Temple. The leader was an average-sized man from the town of Nazareth, an insignificant town north in Galilee.

It was a funny sight, the man riding a donkey's colt, his long legs dangling almost to the ground. The little donkey, skitty and frightened, walked slowly.

The man's followers cheered. Shouts echoed down the hill, across the valley, up toward the city gates. People stopped to stare. The hillside became alive with joy. Citizens and pilgrims joined the group. It was a fantastic parade.

The man was serious, almost sad. Light, airy cheers sounded and hurrahs reverberated. Festival garments were flung on the dusty road. Purple coats, blue scarves, cloaks of green and orange were tossed before the man and donkey. Human voices sang rich "Hosannas" all around.

Voices rang, "Jesus, Jesus, blessed one who comes after King David. Blessed is the one who comes in the name of the Lord. Praise be to God!"

Hosannas sang out as the throng made its way up the sacred hill toward the Temple.

Jesus, the serious, almost sad man, rode the young donkey. Jesus rode on.

(Children enter rear of sanctuary)

CHILDREN: *(Directed by the narrator)* Hosanna! Hosanna! Hosanna! Blessed is Jesus who comes in the name of God! Hosanna! Hosanna! Hosanna!

NARRATOR: God's People, please join me in hosannas. *(Directs the congregation of God's people)* Hosanna! Hosanna! Hosanna!

(Children come dancing and bouncing joyously down the aisles singing "The Earth Sings Praise" and waving helium-filled balloons of many colors, or streamers of colorful cloth. This can be choreographed into a simple dance. Children may be nursery through junior high, if there are few, or elementary children if there are many. They should use their arms, as well as legs, to express exuberance. Children sit)

NARRATOR: How delightful this sight and sound of the Palm Sunday parade must have been. We can only imagine being there. What joy and admiration the people must have felt! The disciples' hearts must have overflowed with exaltation. How grand the procession, as it flowed down the hill outside Jerusalem, and spilled through the valley, and marched in jubilation up to the Temple. It was a time to be glad. A time to praise. Jesus said, if the people had not shouted praise, the inanimate would have become animated with adoration.

We, also, call this Passion Sunday because it marks the beginning of the week of Jesus' pain, suffering and death. Some of the praise may not have been genuine. People may have joined the hosannas not knowing who Jesus was. Some may have just happened to be there, or wanted to vent steam.

Some stood on the sides and scowled as they plotted ways to destroy Jesus.

We may examine our motives as we praise this Palm Sunday. Let's join in singing our praise.

Hymn: "Love Divine, All Loves Excelling"

Prayer *(A youth may prepare one or the following may be used)*

VOICE 1: Dear God, divine mother and father to us, accept our praise. This Sunday we remember the grand parade in honor of Jesus, the Christ. We join together to praise, Dear Living God.

VOICE 2: We remember, too, the passion of Jesus. This is a time to focus on the suffering and pain of holy week. The gospel stories of his time of anguish move us.

VOICE 3: What a gift you have given us, O God, that we are your daughters and sons. How vividly Jesus affirmed that gift in his life, teachings, passion and death. Thank you, God.

ALL: Hosanna, we will praise God. Praise God for the gift of love. Praise God, we receive this gift. Hosanna. Hosanna!

VOICE 1: In our time there are those who suffer, show us ways to bring healing. In our time there are lonely people. There are hungry. There are thirsty. There are those who are imprisoned and who are naked.

VOICE 2: Set us about the task of healing. Show us how to find the wounded. Let us learn to bind their wounds.

VOICE 3: Tender God, open us to receiving food, drink, comfort, covering and freedom, for we, too, are in need.

ALL: Hosanna, Hosanna, Loving God, the stones will shout if we do not offer our praise. Amen.

Hymn: "Tell Me The Stories Of Jesus"
or "All Glory, Laud, and Honor"

Meditation And Reflection: "People in the Palm Sunday Parade"

(Young people may take the topics and prepare their own ideas or use the ideas presented here, adding their own stories or examples, if they wish)

NARRATOR: Now, we will look at some of the kinds of people who were part of the first Palm Sunday Parade. First: Those people who prepared.

FIRST SPEAKER: Before the parade, two of Jesus' disciples were sent ahead to make preparation for the "triumphant entry" into the holy city of Jerusalem. They found an untrained colt of a donkey and brought it for Jesus to ride.
    The prophet Isaiah told about making preparations:

> *In the wilderness prepare the way of the Lord, make straight in the desert a highway for our God.*
>   — Isaiah 40:3

    John the Baptist worked preparing for Jesus' ministry. He was sent before Jesus to make ready. John lived simply, camping out in the Judean wilderness. Crowds came to hear him.
    His message was "change." Repent! Toss away the wasteful parts of your life. Get ready for someone special, someone special sent by God. One day John said, "Here is Jesus. Here he is, God's special one! I am not worthy to untie his shoes."

Those who prepare are not the main event. Their job is to warm up the audience, set up the tent, make the arrangements. They are not the star. They are called to prepare. Isaiah said:

> *How beautiful upon the mountains*
> *are the feet of the messenger*
> *who announces peace,*
> *who brings good news,*
> *who brings salvation,*
> *who says to Zion, "Your God reigns."*
> — Isaiah 52:7

Some made preparation for Jesus.

ALL: The man on the donkey rode on. He rode on.

NARRATOR: There were the people who gave their clothes.

SECOND SPEAKER: In the Palm Sunday parade to honor Jesus, some gave up their coats and parts of their clothing. Their coats may have covered muddy or dusty spots in his path. People placed them on the roadway as a significant sign of admiration. The act of laying them on the path was a gesture of humility. They took the clothes off their backs in the joy of the celebration. This act identified them with Jesus.

Their clothes, lying on the path, could no longer keep off the wet rain or the hot sun. The clothes they smoothed on the road may not have been worn again, but were probably kept and treasured. They were thrown as mementos of the changes brought into their lives by the young man riding on the yearling colt. They were thrown on the path as an act of praise. They lay a colorful "Hosanna."

There were those who gave up their coats for Jesus.

ALL: The man on the donkey rode on. He rode on.

NARRATOR: There were those who sang praise.

THIRD SPEAKER: Many of the people in the parade sang praise. It started from a few. It spread to a multitude. The friends of Jesus knew the tunes and the words. Others joined in. Hosannas drifted from the mouths of children and all ages.

People once blind, who had been healed by Jesus, saw the gay colors of cloth lying on the path. There were those who could not walk until Jesus came; they danced along the way. Praise would not stay in their throats; it leaked out in a pleasing melody.

Perhaps a few sang who would never give their labor, a drop of sweat, or spot of blood for Jesus. They were the follow-the-leader types, who would follow the next leader.

Perhaps, some were too shy to sing. They silently gave praise in their hearts. Their hosannas were real, but unheard. The concert of praise would remain for days, weeks, and years an undercurrent of jubilation bringing continuous joy.

There were those who sang praise.

ALL: The man on the donkey rode on. He rode on.

NARRATOR: There were those who shouted, "Stop it!"

FOURTH SPEAKER: There were some who yelled at Jesus, "Stop it!" Who thought the whole praise parade was silly, overwrought. Who did not want their present order threatened. Who thought it unseemly and undignified!

Goodness, all that noise in the Temple. Someone had to make sure all those dancing, singing children did not get mud on the carpet, or dirty the newly-painted walls . . . Goodness, worship is for adults . . . Stop it! Get those who praise out and this whole unscheduled parade thing stopped. If the city leaders had arranged it, they could control it. This shouting and "hosannaing" was out of control. Spontaneity was not welcomed. A good parade takes lots of careful planning. Such arrangements are made by people who merit the job. Whoever heard of such impropriety? Who did these Galileans think they were? There are officials for taking care of celebrations, especially religious parades! There were people who said, "Stop it!"

ALL: The man on the donkey rode on. He rode on.

NARRATOR: In the Palm Sunday Parade there was a person of honor.

FIFTH SPEAKER: A person of honor rode the donkey. This same man was approved by the Spirit of God at his baptism in the Jordan three years before.

He didn't ride a powerful war horse or in a Cadillac convertible. There was no special color to his robe, no braid or golden trim. His clothes were common and there was no long train.

The man who rode the donkey showed no sign of wealth, or power, or promise. He was an itinerant teacher with a motley group of followers. What could he offer Jerusalem?

This man calmed the dashing waves. He quieted the storm and the stormy anguish in hearts. This man asked people, whom he had healed, to remain silent. Now, he permits these exploding expressions of worship and joy. He commends the children who have recognized that it is time for hosannas. He acknowledges their open reverence. A circle of delight must have visited Jerusalem that wonderful day.

There was Jesus, the Christ, one who was honored.

ALL: The man rode on. The Christ rode on!
May the living Christ ride on in our hearts, our community!

Silent Moments For Meditation *(Narrator may indicate there will be a few moments for silent individual meditation)*

Responsive Reading *(Readers and Congregation)*

VOICE 4: Lift up your heads, O gates!
and be lifted up, O ancient doors!
that the King of glory may come in.

VOICE 5: Who is the King of glory?

PEOPLE: The Lord, strong and mighty,
the Lord, mighty in battle.

VOICE 4: Lift up your heads, O gates!
and be lifted up, O ancient doors!
that the King of glory may come in.

VOICE 5: Who is this King of glory?

PEOPLE: The Lord of hosts,
he is the King of glory. Hosanna! (Psalm 24:7-10)

VOICE 6: Listen! Your sentinels lift up their voices,
together they sing for joy;
for in plain sight they see
the return of the Lord to Zion.

PEOPLE: Break forth together into singing,
you ruins of Jerusalem;
for the Lord has comforted his people,
he has redeemed Jerusalem.
The Lord has bared his holy arm
before the eyes of all the nations;
and all the ends of the earth shall see
the salvation of our God. (Isaiah 52:8-10)

Offering

NARRATOR: One way to praise God is by our offering. Let us give our money to be used for God's glory.

Offertory Music

Offertory Prayer
  Lord, we bring our gifts to acknowledge and celebrate our fellowship of love, begun in creation, demonstrated in Jesus, and expressed in our Christian worship today. Amen.

Doxology *(Children dance and move in praise as they follow the ushers to the back of the sanctuary)*

NARRATOR: *(Offers challenge to the congregation)* Dear People of God, we have celebrated and remembered. May I challenge you to read this week one of the Gospel accounts of Jesus' passion? In your home, or with a friend, share a hymn each day this holy week.

ALL CHILDREN AND YOUTH: Surely now is the day to be saved. This is the day to love. This is the time for rejoicing and praise. People of God, this is the season for drawing near to the Living God. Hosanna! Hosanna! Hosanna!

Hymn: "Come, Christians, Join To Sing"
or "Ask Ye What Great Thing I Know"
or "Rejoice Ye Pure In Heart"

Benediction *(Youth might sing "Sweet, Sweet Spirit" or "Turn Your Eyes Upon Jesus" or the refrain of "Blessed Assurance")*